Self-Preservation
A Survival Guide for a Career in Trauma-Exposed Environments

Maureen Pollard, MSW, RSW

Other books by Maureen Pollard
The Twentieth Year: A Memoir of Miscarriage
Best Interests: A Novel
What I Wish for You (a book of affirmations)

Self-Preservation: A Survival Guide for Work in Trauma-Exposed Environments

Copyright 2024 by Maureen Pollard

Cover painting copyright 2024 by Ron Hawkins

Self Preservation 9 x 12" Acrylic, collage, pencil and marker on birch panel

Cover design copyright 2024 by Maureen Pollard

Book design copyright 2024 by JBJ Editing

Print ISBN 978-1-9991742-6-2

Digital ISBN 978-1-9991742-7-9

Published in Canada.

Pollard, Maureen, author

Self-help/Maureen Pollard

All rights reserved.

No part of this book may be reproduced in any form or by any electronic or mechanical means including information storage and retrieval systems, without permission in writing from the publisher.

No liability is assumed for damages that may result from the use of information contained within. Please consult with your health professional to create a plan for health and wellness that meets your unique needs.

Foreword by Brian Knowler
A Little About Me and How This Guide Came to Be
The Realities
Personal Resilience Factors
Coping With Thoughts
Coping With Feelings
Acceptance of Change
Optimism and Perspective
Control What You Can
Goal Setting
Social Connection
Healthy Boundaries
Humour
Gratitude
Self-Care for the Mind, Body and Spirit
Organizational Resilience Factors
Self-Preservation Strategies
Physical Activity
Breathwork
Grounding and Centering
Relaxation Strategies
Intentional Rest and Play
Sleep Strategies
Vagus Nerve Activation
When Things Go Wrong
Planning for Problems
Debriefing
Recovering Resilience
Making Mistakes and Taking Ownership
Carrying It All
TL;DR Principles of Self-Preservation I Wish Everyone Knew
When It's Time to Leave
Final Notes
Worksheets
SMART Goal Setting

Boundaries
Gratitude
What You Say to Yourself Matters: Affirmations Work
Thoughts, Feelings and Actions: Breaking Negative Patterns
Reframing
Pathways to Stress Release
Resources

Foreword

When I first encountered Maureen Pollard's work, I was struck by her unflinching honesty and deep empathy. As someone who has spent years navigating the labyrinth of mental health from the frontlines of first response—both personally and professionally—her perspective and words resonated with me on a level that few others have. The realities she describes, the challenges she highlights, and the compassion she extends to those in high-stress, trauma-exposed work environments are not just insightful; they're essential. This is not just another guide on resilience; it's a lifeline for those who find themselves in the trenches of human suffering, day in and day out.

Working on the front lines, whether in law enforcement, fire and rescue, healthcare, social work, or any other field where trauma is a constant companion, is not for the faint of heart. The toll it takes is profound, yet it's often underestimated or, worse, ignored. Maureen has a unique way of articulating what so many of us feel but struggle to express—the slow erosion of the self that inevitably comes with witnessing humanity at its most vulnerable.

One of the most powerful aspects of Maureen's approach is her understanding of *sanctuary trauma*. This concept, which she describes in detail, is something that many of us have experienced but couldn't quite put into words. It is, unfortunately, an oft-downplayed piece of the mental health puzzle because it forces organizations to admit that they have, knowingly or not, fostered an environment that is harmful, toxic, or worst of all, apathetic.

When the institutions and people who are supposed to support you instead leave you floundering, it can feel like a betrayal on the deepest level. This book doesn't shy away from that harsh truth. Instead, it confronts it head-on, offering not just recognition, but also strategies for coping and healing.

Maureen's work reminds us that high-stress, trauma-exposed work will change you—it's inevitable. But she also makes it clear that this change doesn't have to mean destruction. Yes, you will never be the same person you were before you walked into this world of pain and suffering.

But you are not broken.

You are not weak.

You are human.

Your reactions—your struggles—are natural.

As someone who has walked a similar path, I can attest to the importance of the strategies Maureen lays out. They are not just theoretical ideas; they are practical tools that can help you maintain your humanity in the face of overwhelming odds. Whether it's finding ways to keep hope and joy alive or creating a self-preservation plan that works for you, these are the kinds of things that can make the difference between surviving and truly living.

It's easy to lose sight of your own worth when you're constantly confronted with the worst that life has to offer. The stories you carry with you can become weights that drag you down, making it hard to see the good parts of the world that are still around you. But Maureen's words are a powerful reminder that you are always worthy of the time and energy it takes to care for yourself; to cut those weights loose when you can. Your wellness is not just a luxury; it's a necessity.

In my own journey, I've found that it's the moments of connection—whether with a book, a person, or even a quiet moment of reflection—that have helped me the most. This book is one of those connections. It's a conversation between Maureen and the reader, filled with understanding, compassion, and a deep respect for the work that you do.

So, as you read this book, I encourage you to take Maureen's advice to heart. Experiment with the strategies she offers. Find what works for you and hold onto it. Because in this line of work, your greatest asset is your resilience, and that resilience needs to be nurtured. It's not just about surviving another day on the job. It's about thriving in a world that often seems determined to break you. It's about recognizing that while the work you do is important, so too is your own health and happiness.

As Maureen says in her Final Notes, 'You shine a beautiful light in this world,' and that light deserves to be protected.

Maureen's book is a gift—a guide to help you navigate the complex and often treacherous waters of trauma-exposed work. It's a reminder that while this work will change you, it doesn't have to destroy you. You can emerge from it stronger, wiser, and more compassionate, not just towards others, but towards yourself as well.

So, as you turn these pages, know that you are not alone. There are others who have walked this path before you, there are those who walk it alongside you now, and there are those who will follow in the trail that you are helping to blaze.

And together, with the wisdom Maureen shares in this book, we can all find a way to keep our light shining brightly, no matter how dark the world around us may seem.

Brian Knowler

A Little About Me and How This Guide Came to Be

I am a registered social worker, with a private practice in a small town in central Ontario, Canada. My career began in 1991 during my final undergraduate year when I was hired to work as an emergency after hours worker for a child protection agency in southern Ontario.

I say that's when my career began because I don't feel my unpaid internships in a youth shelter in Detroit, Michigan, and a locked psychiatric unit in southern Ontario, count, even though that field placement in Detroit is still the item on my resume that draws the most attention in interviews.

I spent twenty years on the front lines of child welfare in a rural county in central Ontario, ten of which included working on high conflict custody and access files across central and southern Ontario. In my private practice, I specialize in supporting people as they adapt traumatic experiences and integrate loss in their lives.

I began speaking about resilience and self care soon after I shifted into private practice. When I learned about compassion fatigue and the impact of working in high stress, trauma-exposed environments, I began to heal my own wounds. As I discovered pathways to healing, I wanted to share hope with others.

I have had the privilege of speaking with audiences across Canada and the United States about the importance of personal resilience and self-preservation across a career. In my adventures, it occurred to me that a guide such as this might have the ability to reach a wider audience. I want this to be simple, straightforward, and practical; an easy read with even easier to implement strategies that may support healing and wellness when our work inevitably puts stress and trauma upon our caring heart.

With warm wishes for your well-being,

Maureen

The Realities

Working on the front lines means that you will walk into other people's trauma several times a shift. You're the one they call, or bring themselves to, when the very worst that can happen to humanity has happened to them. You're trained, you have knowledge and skills, and you have access to tools and resources that can help.

Choosing this work means that you will inevitably experience stress and trauma. You will experience acute stress when there are more calls than you can possibly respond to in a moment, an hour, a shift. You will experience cumulative stress as you encounter, and work to resolve, crisis after crisis. You will experience trauma indirectly and vicariously as you witness events unfold in front of you, take statements about events, read notes and view photographs and other evidence.

Sometimes, the trauma will impact you directly when the situation somehow gets personal. There is a list that is sometimes known as The Terrible Ten, and it identifies the situations most likely to traumatize even the most seasoned veteran in the field. The list includes events such as the on-duty death of a colleague, the suicide of a colleague, high threat situations involving weapons and hostages, incidents involving children, scenes where the responder knows the victim, mass casualty situations, and events with a high level of media coverage. Any of these hold the potential for significant personal impact on those responding.

Sometimes, you'll be impacted by a traumatic incident, or you'll suffer the consequences of a buildup of stress over time. When you're honest about the symptoms – or when you just can't hide them anymore – you may experience judgment, rejection, and sometimes targeted harassment from colleagues and leadership. We call this sanctuary trauma, when the people who are supposed to have your back leave you to flail or cut you loose when you are wounded and struggling.

Stigma is real. When you've been injured and you're working through recovery, it's common to experience assumptions and judgment from family, friends, and community members as well as colleagues. People who haven't lived through what you have don't understand. Those who have similar exposure may be afraid if it could happen to you, it might happen to them. Either way, the landscapes of your friendships will change as some people back away while you're struggling.

It wears you down, all of it: the constant exposure to pain and suffering, and the very real limits to what can be done to help people. Our systems are built upon a foundation of colonialism and patriarchy, woven through with racism, sexism, ableism and all the many ways humans harm one another. From this foundation, the very systems that are proposed to help people in fact harm everyone: the people they are intended to serve, and the people who sign up for service with a desire to serve.

Language evolves, and so sometimes we talk about compassion fatigue, or empathy fatigue, or burnout and we blend the definitions, then separate the experiences out again. Whatever words we use, the experience is real. This work of trying to help create and maintain public health and safety takes a toll on the humans who go to work each shift with the intention to help make things safe and right in the world.

A new recruit can go from wide-eyed to weary-eyed much faster than one might expect. The feeling when entering the field in that first paid position is often one of adventure, if not quite excitement. If they know a little bit about what they're about to be exposed to on the job, it may be a sense of wary anticipation that carries them forward. Still, people are rarely truly prepared for the work they are about to do. It's hard to imagine the sights and smells you'll encounter, and very hard to believe the stories you'll witness and participate in. Sensory details, seemingly insignificant at the time, become yours and remain with you long after you've left a scene. It's not the same as reading a novel or watching a movie or a drama series. Fiction must make sense for people to buy it; real life trauma is messy, chaotic, strange, and unbelievable. It's no wonder new recruits experience shock.

This guide isn't about digging into these realities. This very short section is just about all I'm going to say on the matter of how humans are inevitably wounded in this work. There are some very excellent works already published on those aspects, and if you're interested, you'll find a bibliography with suggested reading in Appendix A.

Instead, this guide is about how to develop, protect, and recover resilience when you work on the front lines, with practical strategies for self-preservation across a career. May it offer you some potential pathways to finding peace amid the chaos and strain of high stress, trauma-exposed work.

Personal Resilience Factors

Resilience is the ability to adapt in the face of adversity, trauma, and stress.
(Road to Resilience, APA, 2015)

This guide will discuss a range of practical strategies an individual can apply to help deal with the inevitable experiences of adversity, trauma, and stress. I want to acknowledge that developing new habits and applying what you learn about personal resilience factors won't help to decolonize the systems that we work within, combat the racism embedded and perpetuated in our structures and through the blind spots of our implicit biases, or dismantle the patriarchy that hurts us all. We work in systems that harm the people the systems are intended to serve as well as the people working within the systems. However, I still believe that the concept of personal resilience is worthy of attention. When we care for our selves, we become grounded, centred, and strong enough to do the work that is required for a better, safer world for everyone.

Personal Resilience Factors	
Coping with Thoughts	Social Connections
Coping with Feelings	Healthy Boundaries
Acceptance of Change	Humour
Optimism and Perspective	Gratitude
Control	Self Care
SMART Goals	

Coping with Thoughts

We can't stop our thoughts. Thoughts are the product of the mind, and the human mind is constantly working. Our brains are trained to notice the negative. We scan the environment for threats as a survival mechanism and are on alert to detect and respond to danger to prevent harm. As a result of this natural tendency, we can end up in negative thought cycles, stuck in our reactions to the perception of impending doom.

When we know this is a common pattern, we can make a conscious decision to counter the experience by challenging the negative assumptions we have learned to make for self-defence. We can notice our automatic thoughts, identify our habitual state of mind, and then retrain ourselves to respond differently to our world.

Considering Alternative Hypotheses.

In every situation that we have a thought about, there may be several possible explanations. When we're able to step back from our initial thought, we can often reduce the stress and prevent reactive behaviour that may cause more problems.

When driving on the freeway, consider how easy it is to be annoyed by someone else's driving habits. It can feel like a personal affront if someone cuts you off or won't let you merge despite your signal. What if you imagine that the driver is on their way to some emergency, that they're in crisis and that's the reason for their poor driving behaviour. When you consider this possibility, and how your own driving skills might be affected if you were in crisis, it can be easier to have empathy for them despite the fear or frustration you felt because of the close call you just had.

It's true, you might still get upset when someone cuts you off. This is a fear response; in the moment it is natural to be afraid there will be an accident, and someone could be hurt or killed. Remind yourself that you're safe and consider possible reasons that the driver could be carelessly hurrying through traffic. You may even find yourself able to send them a wish that everything will be all right when they arrive wherever they're going.

It's true that not every driver who cuts someone off is on their way to a personal emergency, with their fear for a loved one distracting them from safe driving habits. Still, it feels a lot better to consider that alternative hypothesis, to release the fear-based anger and maybe even pay closer attention to your own driving habits.

Challenging Automatic Negative Thoughts.

Automatic negative thinking is also known as cognitive distortion. These thought patterns can become our habitual way of thinking about things, even when our thoughts are not true. It can become difficult to tell the difference between real threats and imagined threats when automatic negative thinking takes over.

Types of Automatic Negative Thinking

Polarization (all or nothing)

Catastrophizing (worst-case scenario)

Overgeneralization (always or never)

Jumping to Conclusions (mind reading or fortune telling)

Personalization (self-blame)

Discounting the Positive (ignoring good things)

Magnification (exaggeration)

Take some time to notice your thoughts. It may be helpful to keep a thought log or a journal to help you identify which of the automatic negative thinking patterns you tend to use most often. Once you're aware of your habits, it becomes easier to manage.

Remember that a thought is not a fact. You have the capacity to reflect on your thoughts and to embrace or release them. Ask what story you're telling yourself about a situation you see as negative. Ask yourself if you may be able to view a situation from a different angle.

Make a list of the negative thoughts you're noticing. Be sure to leave space after each item on your list. Review and reflect on each negative thought. As you think about the situation giving rise to that thought, try using different colour ink to write a challenge thought that is either neutral or positive.

Automatic Thought: I have too much work to do and too many demands on my time.

Challenge Thought: I have many exciting opportunities to choose from.

Coping with Feelings

We all have feelings and none of us can help what we feel. Working in high stress, trauma-exposed environments means that over time you're likely to have some big feelings on the job. These feelings will be layered in with the emotional experiences you'll inevitably have in your personal life.

Learning to Surf

Feelings are often compared to waves. I invite you to imagine that you are standing at the edge of the ocean, wading into the surf. As large waves roll toward you, you learn quickly that trying to stand still and hold your ground will never work. The waves are too powerful. At the least, each wave will pick you up and move you. At worst, a wave will lift and toss you into the depths where your body will slam into rocks and sand, leaving you battered and bruised.

There are other ways to handle the waves. You can prepare for the wave as you see it approaching. Take a deep breath, extend your arms with your hands pointing forward and dive into the wave, taking some control of how you push against this powerful force of nature, which will push back against you.

You can also try to relax your body, letting the wave lift you, carrying you forward with its momentum, before it recedes and leaves you gently drifting in a new place.

If we try to stand strong, ignoring or fighting our feelings, they are likely to batter us. When we dive into our emotions and have a chance to really feel and express them, we can find relief and comfort despite the energy this takes. When we notice our feelings and allow them to carry us a little way with each wave, we can gain perspective and healing.

Expressing with Art

It's always helpful to have outlets for our feelings. We can vent them by talking about what's happening to us with someone trustworthy, who is available and able to listen with compassion. We can also move our feelings through us with physical movement that can help discharge tension. Sometimes talking doesn't feel like enough, or maybe we don't have words, or maybe we're limited in our ability to move, or we're still grappling with difficult emotions after whatever physical activity we've done. When this is true, expressive arts can be a powerful way to move feelings out into the world, often creating brilliant beauty from our deepest pain.

In the book *Bittersweet: How Sorrow and Longing Make Us Whole*, author Susan Cain identifies the quest to transform pain into beauty as one of the greatest catalysts of creative expression, as she asks: "What if we simply took whatever pain we couldn't get rid of and turned it into something else?" and answers her question by saying: "We could write, act, study, cook, dance, compose music, do improv, or decorate. Whether we do these things 'well' is beside the point."

Lessons in the various arts are accessible in person and online, ranging from free introductions to affordable group classes, to private sessions and expensive courses. If you're stuck in difficult feelings, it may be worth exploring your creative side to shift your inner landscape. Learn how to write songs, or paint with watercolour or acrylics. Sign up for a dance lesson or an improv group. Begin journaling using some combination of words, drawing, and collage to tell your story. You may find it brings great relief to have a socially acceptable place to put the biggest feelings you're carrying.

Movement is Medicine

Physical activity gives our nervous system the opportunity to discharge tension. When we're deep in big feelings, it can be helpful to engage our muscles. Go for a walk or a run, put on some music and dance, clean the house, get out on your bike, chop some firewood, or whatever movement feels good to you.

If you can, get outside in nature to move your body. Find a path or hiking trail near your home. Create a garden in your yard or in containers on your balcony. Put your bare feet on the ground. Lift your gaze to the sky. Soak in the sun and feel the breeze on your face.

The thing about feelings is they never last. When you give yourself permission to notice, name and feel them, even the most powerful feelings usually pass within two minutes.

Acceptance of Change

Change is an inevitable fact of life. We begin changing the moment we are conceived, and we change repeatedly as long as we exist. Some of us would prefer to avoid change and do everything in our power to keep things the same for as long as possible. Others are change seekers and chase after new opportunities, people, places, and things to satisfy our craving for variety. Many people fall somewhere in between these two extremes.

As a change avoider, you may prefer your own comfortable space and your usual predictable routines. Change may bring distress and throw you into a bad mood.

If you're someone who prefers to avoid change, it's good to remind yourself that, like it or not, change is coming. If you remember this, you can prepare yourself for the experience of change. It can help if you anticipate the change, even if you will mourn.

If you're a change seeker, you may always be looking for the next great thing. You may feel bored with routines and find yourself ruminating when things stay the same.

If you're someone who seeks change, it's good to check in with yourself about whether you're moving with pleasure toward a new opportunity or recoiling with fear and pain as you try to escape something you might need to face and heal from.

Optimism and Perspective

Optimism can be defined as the ability to see the potential positive in any situation. Perhaps even more than the ability, it's having the tendency to see the potential positive side.

Optimism is a factor in resilience, in part because it has an impact on how we think. Remember, how we think is one of the two things we can control. So, if we tend to be optimistic, we are likely to be more resilient. An optimist spends enough time seeing the bright side that they become able to do so in almost any situation.

Some of us are born with a sunny disposition, optimists at heart. It's not necessary, though; optimism can be learned. We can train ourselves to look for the best in any circumstance; the more you seek it out, the more apparent it is to you in everyday situations.

There are so many songs about optimism, hope, and encouragement available. Some of my favourites include "It's Okay" by Alan Doyle, "Gonna Be Okay" by Brent Morgan, "Bound to be Okay" by Mike Evin, "It's Okay" by Nightbirde, "Shine Your Light" by the Ennis Sisters, and the iconic "Always Look on the Bright Side of Life" by Monty Python. You'll find these along with songs from other genres on the Spotify Playlist I made. There's a QR code with the link on the resources page at the end of the book.

You can also create your own personalized playlist with songs you know will lift your mood when you need it.

Optimism is not about the idea that everything will always be fine if we just think happy thoughts; that's just not true. Those who work in high stress trauma-exposed environments know better than most that sometimes, in the moment, nothing is fine at all. We can remind ourselves and one another that even when things are going wrong, everything passes and things will go right again.

Optimism is about the idea that even in the very darkest of times and the most traumatic tragedies, the human spirit can heal from wounds. We can look at a situation and say, "This is horrific," and we can then reflect and say, "I can find a way to go on."

Blind optimism in the face of any circumstance is not helpful. Realistic optimism is the key, which brings us to the idea of perspective. When we have the ability to pause, to breathe through a difficult moment, we can find a way to see potential solutions. We can hold hope.

Perspective. It's how we find a way to concentrate on the details even as we hold the big picture in our mind, and it's easier said than done.

You've likely heard the expression, "The glass is half full (or half empty)." This concept is often used to try to explain optimism. But the realist, who has perspective and understands a bigger picture, can say that the glass is actually full at all times – half full of a liquid and half full of air.

Keeping perspective helps us to stay in the present moment more often. We can find ourselves ruminating on things that happened in the past and can't be changed, or fretting about things that may or may not happen in the future. When we remember that our power lies in the present moment, we can reduce our distress. Remind yourself you are safe here now, and you can act – or rest – in this moment. That is all you can do, and it is enough.

Control What You Can

Often, when we've chosen to work in a profession that involves showing up to help people through life's challenges and tragedies, it's because we've become used to being in control. We may have learned at a young age that things went better – or at least felt better – if we figured out what needed to be done, took charge and got it done. We're sometimes described as having Type A personalities, having a good eye for detail, and we may be defined by our drive and commitment.

The reality is that there are very few things in life we can control, even if we're highly organized, driven and accomplished. We can't truly control people, environments, and events. What looks like control is really just reacting or responding to situations as they arise.

We do have some control over two things: how we think about someone or something, and what action we personally take in a situation. When we remember this, we can turn our focus inward and find our way through even very difficult situations.

How we think can really have an impact on how we feel and how we behave. It's so easy to get caught up in negative thought patterns where we criticize others or imagine catastrophe and worst-case-scenarios. When we're in such a state of mind, our feelings of pain and fear can rise, often expressed as anger, which we know is more powerful than the vulnerable feelings that arise when we are hurt and afraid. This emotional response to our thought patterns can create behaviour changes that interfere with our relationships and our personal well-being as we struggle to cope with difficult experiences.

When we change our thinking, we can have a significant change in our experience of the world.

Reframing

Like the concept of challenge thoughts, reframing allows us to step back and consider a worry or a frustrating situation from different perspectives. We can neutralize worry or frustration or even consider the potential for positivity.

For example, if we are worried that it's going to rain and we can't walk outside, we can reframe this thought to consider that the garden needs rain, and we can dance inside. Alternately, we can dress for the rain, remembering that there is no such thing as bad weather, only the wrong clothing.

Ultimately, you're acknowledging that your concern may be valid, but you're also actively working to find a positive way to view the current situation. Such thinking strategies help us keep our perspective and help prevent us from being dragged into a low mood or foul temper when we're faced with challenges.

This type of work isn't the same as the idea that we can "think happy thoughts and everything will be fine." Sometimes, as we well know in the work of public health and safety, everything will not be "fine", although people do adjust in the wake of tragedy. Often, everything will be changed forever, and the people involved in a situation will struggle to adapt to the experience of grief and trauma. So, it's not about ignoring facts, or pretending, or denial. It's about looking at a situation from all angles in the effort to find some positive aspect that we can focus on and build from there.

The ability to turn our thoughts to such possibilities means that we'll be able to move forward with the second thing that we can control: what action we personally take. When you can think about positive potential, you can take some small action toward the desired outcome.

For example, you may not be able to control what time your workday starts. There's often a schedule and everyone rotates through in turn. What you can control is how you think about it, and what steps you take to prepare for your shift.

If you're scheduled to start at 7:00 a.m., you have some choices to make about how you spend your time before your shift starts. If you're an early riser, that may mean waking at 5:00 a.m., taking time for a workout, shower, and breakfast before you head to work. If you're not really a morning person, you may decide to live close to your workplace, to shower and prep your lunch before bed, wake up late and grab a protein bar on your way out the door to work. It's true, you may not be able to control what time you start work, but you truly have a lot of control about how you prepare and get there.

We are confronted daily by the things we can't control or change. Resilience comes from our ability to recognize and take control of what we can.

You might use a calendar, day planner, or scheduling app to create a plan for your time. Acknowledge your patterns and preferences, and work with them instead of fighting the flow. Early risers can block time before work for important tasks, including self care, while night owls can schedule activities in the evenings when their energy is highest. What's most important is finding the plan that meets your needs and helps you function at your best.

Goal Setting

It's true that setting goals can help us to achieve great things. It's also true that setting goals can challenge us and lead to frustration, sometimes even immobilizing us in the pursuit of those great things.

The key to effective goal setting lies in the decisions you make about each specific goal. When you have one broad, vague goal, it's easy to get lost in the process and hard to make progress. When you break that larger goal down into small steps and stages, it suddenly becomes more accessible. You can imagine completing one task at a time, which helps motivate you to take the steps. You can celebrate small successes along the way to the overall target and these wins help fuel your forward motion.

One proven strategy for goal attainment involves setting SMART goals.

1. Be **S**pecific.
2. Make it **M**easurable.
3. Make sure it's **A**chievable.
4. Choose **R**elevant tasks.
5. Set a **T**imeframe for completion.

When you use this method, it makes it easier to know just what you should be doing, and you'll know whether you've done it or not. Setting time frames can help with planning and motivate you to stay on track.

As an example, if you want better work/life balance, you can choose to set a boundary around the time and energy you spend on work. You may decide to stop answering voice messages and email after the end of your shift and use the Do Not Disturb function on your device for the hours you'll be asleep, or on your days off. While it's true that this can be difficult in a job where you work shift work or must be on call for emergencies, it's also true that you can likely find at least a few hours a week or a few days a month to take a hiatus from the endless demands of voice messages and email.

Social Connection

We're wired to connect with others; humans thrive in relationships, and this is true for introverts and extroverts alike. Extroverts need more interaction with other people, which they find energizing and restorative. They may have many connections with family and friends, ranging from deep, close relationships to superficial acquaintances. Introverts need more time alone to recover after socializing. Although their relationships may be less in number, they tend to be deep connections, whether with family or friends. Either way, all people need some sense of connection to others as part of finding balance and maintaining wellness.

At Work

Working on the front lines, social connections are vital to wellness. It can be very helpful to have connections with colleagues and peers who do the same type of work that you do. These are people who understand what it's like to routinely be exposed to stress and trauma as part of a typical workday. You may develop relationships with people you meet in school, at work, in your community, or within your family. Relationships with others in the field help you feel seen, heard, and understood in the work you do. Consider eating together during break times, form a lunchtime walking group or a book club, or celebrate one another's birthdays with a social event. Getting to know each other in these ways can strengthen relationships at work and help your team to feel more supported.

While these relationships can be very supportive, it's also true that some of our connections at work can become toxic, rife with negativity. When we are surrounded by people who are stuck in frustration, distrust, pain and pessimism, it's easy to fall into habits of resentment and complaints. While it can be validating to vent your feelings to someone who gets it, it can easily drag everyone down if the conversations focus only on the challenges of the work environment, the leadership, colleagues or the work itself. If you notice these patterns, it may be time to withdraw a bit from some of these relationships to reconnect with what you enjoy about your career.

At Home and in the Community

It's equally important to have relationships with family and friends outside of work. These relationships can be set aside when we find ourselves absorbed by our work, functioning with different schedules due to shift work or taking on overtime.

Family relationships can be challenging at times, too. Every family member brings their individual experience, personality, and temperament to the relationship. Spending time with family can be a safe haven. This may be especially true if other family members are engaged in similar work on the front lines of public health and safety. Even when that's not the case, family will often accept and support us because of the shared bond that is, sometimes, deep and loving. This is true of our family of origin, as well as the family we create with a partner.

Sometimes the people we're related to by genetics are not safe. When this happens, and the relationships are strained or non-existent, we have the option to create what's sometimes known as "chosen family". These may be people in your life who you become close to, where the bond becomes similar to what one might think of in a biological family. We may informally adopt parents or grandparents, and we may have "sisters of the heart" and "brothers from another mother". These relationships can be very adaptive, providing support and connection to people who accept and support us. Of course, these folks may stand in for our family of origin, or we may have some of these folks in our circle in addition to healthy biological family connections.

Aside from family and family-like relationships, developing and maintaining friendships with people who have experience quite different than yours can help you maintain perspective, which we learned earlier is a valuable factor in resilience. Having a variety of relationships, activities, and hobbies can give us new perspectives and help keep us feeling fresh by giving us a break from being continuously immersed in our workplace environment and mindset. If you're not already involved in a community group, consider joining a local activity or club that appeals to you. If you've always wanted to try a new hobby or sport, or get re-engaged in an old favourite, this is a great way to make connections outside of work with people who share your other interests.

Healthy Boundaries

People who work on the frontlines of health and public safety are often good organizers, pay attention to detail, and agree to look after things for people. We say yes and we step up to get the job done. People are counting on us at work, across our community, and at home. We want to make sure it gets done, and it gets done right.

Over time, we discover that saying "Yes" to others can contribute to fatigue, leaving us struggling to find time and energy to meet our own needs. The ability to say "No" or "Not right now" is an important aspect of self-preservation. You can choose what you agree to, although sometimes it is hard to say no to others. Saying "Yes" to yourself is an important aspect of resilience. Setting boundaries to protect your energy helps extend your longevity and improves your on-going ability to provide excellent care for others.

Consider the ways you spend your time. What are your responsibilities, routines, and obligations? Make a chart like this one and identify all the tasks that fill your day in one of the three columns.

What Nourishes Me?	What Must Get Done?	What Depletes Me?
Songwriting	Feeding pets	Committee meetings
Running	Laundry	Weeding gardens
Herbal tea	Grocery shopping	Paperwork

Once you've sorted your activities like this, carefully consider whether anything in the categories of what must get done or what depletes you could be delegated or done less often. Even a small change can open a bit more time in your busy schedule for an activity that rejuvenates you. You might also find that some of the things you find nourishing take little enough time that you can fit them into your plans. For example, if you have a favourite hot beverage, you can bring it to your next committee meeting, giving you the soothing feel, aroma, and taste to enjoy while the committee moves through its agenda.

Healthy boundaries also mean recognizing our physical and mental limits when it comes to work. It often feels like there are never enough hands to do all that needs doing, and that time is fleeting. It's easy to stay late, come in early, or handle being called in times of crisis – which can happen all the time. This isn't sustainable, though. If you don't recognize your limits, you will certainly find yourself struggling at some point with fatigue, distress, and illness.

It's important to establish boundaries for your time off work. Leave the building when your workday is done. Establish times of the day or days of the week when you use the Do Not Disturb function on your phone, or the automated out of office message in your email system. Take time for your lunch and breaks throughout the day, even if you must make it work at odd times. Schedule activities you enjoy with people you like during your time off. Plan – and take – vacations every year.

Serenity Prayer for Caregivers

Grant me the Serenity to prioritize the things I cannot delegate,
The Courage to say no when I need to, and
The Wisdom to know when to go home.
Author unknown

Humour

Humour is a survival skill. When we face the most horrific, terrifying, and graphic experiences humans can go through, we are shocked. Over and over, our system is confronted and reverberates with reaction as we show up and do what must be done in the aftermath of a crisis. Even when we have done this work for years, our system will still receive a jolt each time we attend a new scene and take in new sights, sounds, and smells that get added to the macabre collection of memories we carry because of our work.

It is no surprise that our minds sometimes rebel. Being human can be surprising and weird. This is true in life and in death, in times of peaceful calm and in times of chaotic crisis. Absurdities abound in this life and can make us laugh. As a result, it's completely normal to develop a morbid sense of humour over the course of a career where you are continually confronted with the absurdities of calamity, disaster, and death.

We laugh, sometimes to deny the grim realities. We laugh because we are overwhelmed. We laugh because it gives us a release, not unlike the release we get from a good cry. Sometimes we laugh to keep from crying when we find ourselves witness to the strangeness of it all. It's true, after all, that truth is stranger than fiction. The audience for fiction expects that a story will unfold in an orderly fashion, while the truth of real life has no such obligation.

I regularly normalize this morbid sense of humour when I speak to individuals and groups about resilience. You are not broken; you are just having a natural human response to your experience. It's important to be mindful of your audience, though. These moments of laughter at grim absurdities are windows into experiences that many people remain blissfully unaware of because you do your job, and they don't have to see what you see or know what you know. They are not prepared for the realities and won't understand what's so funny.

Humour can give us respite and help us shift from pain to a more neutral mindset in the face of difficulties. We can purposefully seek out laughter as medicine when we are struggling. During difficult times, a funny movie or a favourite comedian can bring on a laugh to help counteract the heavy feelings we are struggling with. If only for an hour or two, you can set aside your worries and be in silliness.

Laughter yoga is a thing, too. Beginning with exercises that mimic the movements our bodies make in laughter; one is gently guided into a physical experience that begins with breathing and guided muscle movement and usually ends with genuine laughter.

A good belly laugh, the freedom to just release a burst of energy in this lighthearted way, can give us a boost. Find ways to invite laughter into your life as a pathway into the light when darkness hovers all around. Let yourself laugh as a way through it all.

Gratitude

The ability to bounce back from adversity, trauma and stress is enhanced when we can remind ourselves of the good things in our lives. Remember, our brains are excellent at detecting danger and negative situations. This ability to notice and deal with threats is part of our survival mechanism that can become a habit that makes it harder to remember there is still good in this world when we work with people during their most difficult times.

Actively taking time each day to notice the things you are grateful for is an important factor in resilience. When you turn your attention to the people, places, and things you appreciate, it helps change your outlook, offering relief and feelings of pleasure. Even on the darkest day, it is possible to find things that you feel grateful for. In fact, it is often on those most difficult days that we most need to focus on something that will lift our spirits.

Three Good Things Challenge

Using a small journal that appeals to you and a comfortable pen, set aside a few minutes each day to write a list of things that you are grateful for. You might choose to write three things every day, or you might just write what comes to mind, noting three things one day and listing just one or as many as ten good things the next. Whatever time of day you choose and however many items on your list, this gratitude practice will work to train your brain over time to notice the good things in your life. You'll find this practice also works if you just take time to turn your mind to the gratitude you feel, even without writing it down.

52 Card Thank You Challenge

Pick up a few packages of thank you cards you like. Keep them somewhere handy, along with some stamps. Whenever someone has done something you appreciate, or you have positive thoughts about someone in your life, write them a short thank you note. Address the envelope and add the stamp right away to increase the likelihood you will send this small but important message of gratitude.

Thank you notes are a small but effective way to boost your resilience. Like firewood warms you three times – when you cut it, when you split and stack it, and when it burns – thank you notes have the potential to warm you when you think of the person you appreciate, when you write the note and deliver it, and when you sometimes receive the person's pleasant response. As a bonus, this gratitude practice will help strengthen your social support network.

Self Care for the Mind, Body, and Spirit

A basketball bounces best when it is in good condition and filled with air. A car drives best when it is well-maintained and fuelled. Helping professionals provide excellent care when they have first taken good care of themselves!

Self care means prioritizing care of your mind, body, and spirit. The mind is nourished by making connections to new learning, checking your perspective, and managing your thoughts and feelings as part of mental wellness. Taking care of your body is both as simple and as complicated as getting a good night's rest, eating nutritious food, and moving your body in ways that keep you limber and healthy.

Your spirit flourishes by finding meaning and purpose in life and allowing yourself to feel joy and peace.

All these aspects of wellness are important to tend to in a proactive routine designed to keep you healthy. When you notice your warning signs, it's time to contemplate additional self care strategies to counteract your natural reaction to either prolonged exposure to stress or an acute crisis you may face.

How do you know if you're struggling? Think about the ways you hold tension in your body. Consider the way you behave when you are rested and calm, and the ways that changes when you're dealing with stressful situations. Notice if it seems harder to manage negative thoughts. When you know your warning signs, you can engage in self care.

Making time in a busy schedule for some of these simple strategies for building and maintaining resilience can increase satisfaction with work and life, improving overall well-being and longevity throughout your career and beyond.

__Sleep:__ Follow good sleep hygiene practices to support your ability to fall asleep, stay asleep, get back to sleep if you wake in the night and to rise feeling well-rested.

__Hydration:__ Drink water regularly. Keep a pitcher of water infused with your favourite fruit in the fridge. Find an herbal tea you enjoy for those times when you need a hot beverage but don't need caffeine.

__Nutrition:__ Choose foods you enjoy. Chop some vegetables and fruit for the week. Cook a large batch of a meal or two you love and store them in single serving portions for lunches.

Exercise: Get outside if you can. Play music that inspires you and walk or dance to the beat. Stretch your muscles as you breathe deeply. Even a few minutes will give you a boost.

Intellect: Keep learning. Find workshops or courses that engage your interest and develop your skills. Try hobbies and activities that look like fun. New learning helps us feel fresh, even after years in the field.

Spirituality: Spend time in nature. Find a church community you appreciate. Contemplate the mysteries of the universe. Whatever activity soothes and energizes your soul is good for the spirit.

Taking care of YOU
means the people in your life receive the best of you,
not what's left of you.
Carl Bryan

Organizational Resilience Factors

It's true that individual resilience is an important aspect of wellness. It's also true that individual wellness plans are simply not enough in the face of toxicity in the workplace. An organization that wants to thrive needs to take care of factors that influence resilience at all levels.

This is where we can begin to make a difference on a larger scale. We can implement policy and procedures and create a culture that embraces decolonization, actively engages in anti-racism, and dismantles the patriarchal structures that have harmed so many people.

Resilient Leadership

Are your leaders taking care of themselves, developing self-preservation strategies, and personal wellness plans? If not, they are unlikely to encourage or support their teams in making wellness a priority and this will ultimately create a cycle of burnout, contributing to increased sick time, a greater likelihood of mistakes happening, and high staff turnover rates.

When an organization values resilience, the leadership sets the tone and creates a safer environment for team members to manage their responses to the experiences of stress and trauma. By acknowledging that grief, as well as stress and trauma responses are a natural part of this work, people can begin to create opportunities to prevent harm, and to mitigate harm when incidents happen.

Resilient leadership takes responsibility for creating a "Culture of Caring", in which there are resources and supports designed to take care of the people who are expected to care for so many others in the community in the most difficult situations.

A culture of caring involves the development of a peer support program and access to professional support through resources such as Employee and Family Assistance Programs to help people through the challenges that can happen in life. It can also be helpful to ensure access to specialised trauma care, including the support of a critical incident response team to help in the case of exposure to a traumatic incident on the job.

The provision of staff or outside resources trained to offer effective support is important, and so is having a suitable private space to talk about the challenges as they arise. A meeting room can serve this purpose, but where space permits, it can be quite helpful to have a quiet room that is private, comfortably furnished, and supplied with water and tissues. Some organizations create a wellness space that includes a couch, pillow, and blanket that might allow an employee with a headache to lie down on a lunch break for some relief. Such spaces send the message to team members that they are each valued as a whole person and cared for when they are struggling physically or emotionally and not just when they are at their peak performance.

These provisions are valuable, but without the opportunity to connect with one another throughout the workday, no effective peer support network can be established. Additionally, people need permission to talk about the things that are heavy and hard to deal with in a way that is open, direct, and honest if they're going to find any relief from the pain and fear that arise naturally during a high stress, trauma-exposed career.

A culture of caring extends to the way that people are managed. Leadership that provides education, support, and guidance in the form of supervision for employees creates an environment where team members know they are not alone. It's natural for new, less experienced employees to require more supervision with a logical decrease in supervision over the course of a career. Even senior employees benefit from supervision, as this process offers an opportunity to debrief challenging situations and to brainstorm strategies for success. Ideally, supervision is an opportunity for learning and support as much as a time for direction and correction.

Resilient organizations ensure that staff at all levels have opportunities for on-going training and professional development. It's often necessary to schedule recertification sessions for first aid and other such routine aspects of the job. It's also beneficial to ensure that advanced training on relevant and interesting topics is offered to everyone. Sometimes it's easy to focus training on new employees and those with less experience, but senior staff can also benefit from learning opportunities that keep them fresh and engaged in developments across the field. When we limit training for experienced staff because they already know so much and manage the job just fine, we risk leaving them feeling left out or taken for granted. We also risk creating a rift between senior staff and newer members of the team.

Workload management can be unpredictable and hard to balance on the front lines. There may be trends in terms of busy times over the course of a shift and across the changing seasons throughout the year. In many high stress, trauma-exposed work environments the work is strictly crisis management with ebbs and flows in volume and severity of incidents or cases. As a result, this can be one of the most difficult aspects of organizational resilience to manage. It can help to plan shifts in a balanced way across the team, and it can help to plan vacation or training days throughout the year as well, but we all know that a plan is just an invitation for challenges and change! Although these challenges to workload management are real and inevitable, it's still worth turning our mind to this concept if we are working to create a resilient organization with a culture of caring.

Culture of Caring	
Peer Support & EFAP	Supervision
Safe Place to Talk	Training
Network / Permission	Workload

Clarity of Purpose and Unity in Purpose

What is the purpose of your organization? What is the purpose of your team in relation to the purpose of the organization? In some cases, this will be very clear.

Many organizations have a mission and vision statement that clearly defines the purpose of the organization, and each team within the organization has clear roles and responsibilities. There is a job to do, and everyone on the team works toward the same goals.

This sense of clarity and unity can be enhanced by good communication of policies, procedures, and initiatives. This is particularly important when bringing new people into the organization, and when the organization is undergoing changes that impact the purpose or the functioning of the teams to meet the purpose.

Engagement

Are people involved in decision making? Are they engaged in the work with enthusiasm? What motivates them to get the job done?

When we do things "to" people, or "for" people, it often leads to disinterest, disengagement, and disenfranchisement. People don't feel invested in projects that are foisted upon them, delivered to them in a way that gives them little input or control. Humans don't generally want to feel powerless, which is exactly how these strategies can impact team members.

When your people are involved in the process of making decisions, developing, and executing plans, they are more likely to take an active interest in the work. This kind of engagement also leads to people taking ownership and having pride in the accomplishment of organizational goals.

Collaboration (Internal and External partnerships)

What are relationships like within your organization? Are the teams and departments collaborative or competitive? Do groups function like silos, with little interaction between them?

Internal partnerships can be invaluable in a resilient organization. Good relationships between both team members and departments can help people feel solidarity. It's true that there will always be personality differences, as well as differences in style and habits across the organization. It can be very helpful to ensure teams have training in conflict resolution and problem-solving, and that leadership creates an environment that supports productive communication and transparent solution generation and implementation.

Team building happens when colleagues have opportunities to spend time together engaged in social activities. This might mean a potluck lunch a few times a year to mark the changing of the seasons, a recreational ball tournament, or even something as simple as conversations over coffee in the break room. When people have an opportunity to know each other in casual situations such as these, they are more likely to feel connected and stand together as a team when responding to the next crisis.

What are relationships like between your team and other community organizations? Are there people you work alongside regularly? Are there some groups that you only encounter occasionally?

When there are other community organizations that your team will engage with regularly, it's worth the effort to develop positive, reciprocal relationships whenever possible. Getting to know one another makes it harder to "other" people – treating them as something less than valuable because they're not part of your team or on your "side". Good relationships are likely to lead to a better ability to do good work together as you show up, side-by-side for your community. Consider the possibility of a joint project to benefit the community, or a social activity that would interest both groups. Either of these options will invite the development of friendly, collaborative relationships between organizations that can help when it comes to working together through the challenges on the job.

Self-Preservation Strategies

I used to use the term self-care when I talked about these strategies. We were all talking about it that way – the many things one could do to care for the mind, body, and spirit. It felt luxurious. Who wouldn't want to spend the day at a spa, eat delicious food, get enough sleep, and move their body in ways that feel good? Perhaps because it felt luxurious it was easy to dismiss self care. These basic activities fell to the bottom of the list every time as we tended to all the crises, big and small.

These days, I'm more likely to call it self-preservation. It has more urgency. It feels more like a matter of life and death, and sometimes it is. We don't talk about it often enough, the suicide rates among those on the front lines who sink further and further into the depths of despair, suffering even as they work to relieve the suffering of others.

I want us to all understand that we are worthy of care. That we have needs, and when we meet them, we are more equipped to carry on in a more sustainable way. That these needs are not "one and done" instances, but present themselves, necessary and evolving over time as we learn more, gain experience, and develop the wisdom that often comes with age.

The strategies are simple, and you've likely heard about all of them before in some talk you attended, some book you read, or some conversation you overheard. Simple, yes. That doesn't mean they're easy to implement. Change is hard, and generally a human must be feeling enough pain in their current circumstances that they're willing to consider the unfamiliar and try something different.

When your pain is enough that you're willing to try something different, this section contains some strategies that can help.

Physical Activity (be sure to consult with your physician before beginning any new physical activity)

Stretching

Try hatha yoga, which is gentle, or tai chi, which is sometimes known as "meditation in motion". These activities can give you the opportunity to move your body gently through a range of stretches that will increase flexibility over time.

Strength

Light to moderate weightlifting can be a good way to discharge physical tension and build muscle. Heavy lifting is more demanding, often with a goal of increasing bone strength as well as impacting body composition and improving muscle strength.

Cardio

Aerobic exercise helps improve heart and lung functioning, as well as building strength and stamina. This type of exercise is a good strategy for discharging physical tension as well.

Physiotherapy

This treatment is a proven way to manage and recover from physical injuries using massage, heat, and exercises targeted to improve functioning related to your specific limitations due to injury.

Breathwork

There are a wide range of breathing techniques intended to help regulate the nervous system. Some are slow, deliberate strategies and others are rapid, focused tactics. Each style of breathing will have an impact, and it's a good idea to experiment with a range of options to see which feel most comfortable and useful to you. Once you settle on a couple of preferred breathing strategies, try practicing them a few times a day to develop your technique. If you take three intentional breaths as you are waking up, another three breaths around midday and three more breaths as you are preparing for sleep, you will begin to develop a muscle memory for the breathing strategy that will make it easier to activate when you find yourself in distress and need to breathe to help you manage your response.

For Calm (4-7-8 or intentional breathing)

Inhale as you count to four, then hold your breath for a count of seven, then exhale slowly for a count of eight.

A deep inhalation brings more air into your lungs, and holding your breath allows a longer opportunity for oxygen exchange in the lungs, which allows more oxygenated blood to travel to your brain and muscle tissues. This can help bring clear thinking and relax the muscles which may become tense when there is less oxygen due to the shallow rapid breathing that often occurs when we are in distress. Finally, the long, slow exhale activates the vagus nerve as the air travels across the back of the throat, which releases calming neurotransmitters such as serotonin.

For Focus (4x4 or box breathing)

Inhale as you count to four, hold for a count of four, exhale for four and hold for four.

This steady, consistent pattern of inhalation and exhalation calms the nervous system like the 4-7-8 technique and allows the mind to focus.

For Alertness (breath of fire)

Inhale passively and then exhale forcefully for the same length of time, contracting the stomach muscles to push out the air. Repeat without pause or holding between inhalation and exhalations.

This technique can be used to reduce stress and increase a sense of alertness when one is becoming fatigued. With this pattern you bring oxygen into your system in a more rapid manner than with 4-7-8 or 4x4 breathing, and this rapid exchange with the use of the diaphragm may help with attention, memory, and reaction time.

Grounding and Centering

When we're in distress, our mind is often falling back into ruminating on what is already done, or rushing forward to fret over what might never come to be. We can get caught in these thought loops and our thoughts and feelings can spiral out of control. There are several useful strategies to bring you right back to this present moment, where you are safe, here, now. Generally speaking, our senses are the pathway to the present.

When you notice that familiar feeling of the spiral beginning, try to use your senses to notice your body in its current location. What do you see in the space around you? In the distance? What do you hear? Do you smell any specific scent, or perhaps a blend? What textures can you feel? What is the temperature? Is there a taste in this moment?

As you bring yourself into your body to assess your surroundings using your senses, you are interrupting the distressing thoughts that were beginning to drag you into the spiral. You are reminding your survival centre that you are here now, and safe; there is no need to be on high alert. You can remind yourself – out loud or in your mind – that the past is over, and you are not there anymore.

When distress is acute and extreme, it may take more drastic measures to bring you back to the present moment. I have placed objects, such as an ice cube, into a person's hand, closing my hand over theirs while speaking in a calm, steady voice as I invite them to notice what they are feeling in their hand. I may describe it for them, which helps them focus on the physical sensation and on the sound of my voice. I invite them to take a deep breath now and again as they focus on the feeling in their hand, and I breathe along with them to encourage a deep inhale and a long slow exhale.

Such methods can interrupt intrusive thoughts, flashbacks, and hysterical responses to the shock and raw pain of a trauma.

There are other grounding strategies, such as playing alphabet or word games, reciting poetry, or doing math exercises like counting backwards from 100 by ones, threes, or sevens. Mental strategies such as these also disrupt the negative thought patterns that are associated with distress with a positive, or at least neutral, distraction from the disturbing thoughts and memories.

Physical grounding exercises can include the act of holding something that feels comforting, such as a blanket or object that soothes you. Similarly, you can move yourself into a space that feels comforting physically. Perhaps there is a room in your home that you design as a calming space. Choose a colour for the walls that you find peaceful, furnish the room with a comfortable chair that you can relax into, and bring in a few objects that will contribute to this intentionally soothing environment.

Moving the body is also a useful way to ground yourself in the present. Stretching, taking a walk or run, dancing, or even cleaning your home are all examples of healthy ways to move to allow the feelings of tension and distress to move out of your body. As you move through space and time in whatever way feels good for your body, you may find yourself right here in the present moment feeling your feet on the ground and the air on your skin.

Relaxation Strategies

Tension is a natural response to the experience of stress and trauma. Purposeful relaxation is a natural effort to reduce tension.

Meditation is a proven strategy to reduce tension and encourage relaxation. However, the idea of meditation is often rejected by those who are active, with busy minds and hectic schedules. It can feel intolerable to sit still and impossible to clear the mind. If we expand our concept of meditation, it becomes more accessible. There are a variety of activities that can be considered meditative, and which can help with relaxation.

Some people are able to sit in a comfortable position and focus on clearing the mind with help from a mantra. A mantra is a word, phrase, or sound that is repeated, with the intention of aiding concentration. This is the activity people often think of when asked to meditate. It can feel intimidating to begin and frustrating to try to maintain.

Guided meditations are available through several apps and on the internet. You can find recordings of varying lengths from two minutes to sixty minutes and beyond. These offerings sometimes include a voice narration on topics such as finding calm or releasing sadness. There may be music in the background, and some of these recordings are primarily soothing music. Listening to a guided meditation can help if you find one that is soothing to you. This may mean listening to several variations before you find a voice and music combination that you enjoy.

It is also possible to meditate on the move. One strategy is to engage in a walking meditation, with or without footwear where the ground is safe enough to walk barefoot. When you are walking, focus your attention on the fall of each foot, the connection, disconnection, and reconnection with the earth that your feet make with each step. Whether you are indoors or outside, this technique can allow a restless skeptic to try meditation in a creative way.

Intentional Rest and Play

These days we're all always very busy with agendas and job descriptions at work, as well as to do lists at home and maybe in our community. It can be a challenge to maintain balance when there is so much to do and so many people are counting on us.

It becomes important to plan rest and play amid the busy schedule of what we must get done. If we don't plan it, it won't happen. If it doesn't happen, eventually we become grim and irritable and we suffer at work and at home. It's worth it to plan rest and play. You're worth it.

Some people play sports. Others weave, knit, or crochet. There are folks who bake and those who read. There are so many ways to play.

An important part of healthy boundaries includes taking time for rest and recovery. Humans need down time to strengthen and heal. This includes taking those coffee breaks, making time for a bite to eat, and maybe venturing on a short walk outdoors at lunch.

It is equally important to have days off each week, and to take vacation each year. When you find yourself envious of others who "have time" for coffee, lunch, and vacations, it may be time to pay attention to meeting your own needs for rest and recovery.

Take a catnap. Find a safe, comfortable position where you can close your eyes, slow your breathing, and enjoy a short, but refreshing nap.

Active Rest

When we think about rest, we often think about the idea of sitting or lying still and maybe sleeping. Sometimes, this isn't possible, or it's not what we need to refresh our energy. Active rest can help at these times.

Active rest involves engaging in activities, such as playing video games, doing jigsaw puzzles or crosswords, or watching a movie. You are resting your mind from your usual worries and stressors with this active distraction, which can help clear your head and allow you to calm your nervous system.

Passive Rest

So often in our busy schedules, we find ourselves with a fresh, hot coffee or tea, we take a few sips and before we know it, we've become distracted, and our beverage has gone cold. Sometimes we reheat it, once, twice, maybe more. Other times we just drink it cold (which is probably how iced coffee was invented!).

Passive rest involves engaging in a soothing sensory activity, like finishing a hot beverage while it's still hot. You might choose a cup of your favourite tea, or broth. Use your favourite mug and sit with both hands wrapped around the mug so that you feel the warmth as you inhale the delicious scent. Sit, sip and take the time to thoroughly enjoy the experience. It will only take a few moments to enjoy this nourishment, and when you're done, you'll feel refreshed and ready to face whatever needs to be done next.

Sleep Strategies

While sleeping, we heal physically, mentally, and emotionally. When we're working shift work, facing medical challenges, under the significant stress of a busy schedule, or facing a crisis, we often struggle to get enough sleep. There are a number of strategies that can help whether the challenge is falling asleep, staying asleep, or getting quality sleep.

Environment

It's important to have a safe and comfortable space for sleeping. Choosing soothing colours for the décor can help set the mood for a calm experience in the bedroom. Your bed is an important investment. Having a mattress that suits your body and sleep style can mean the difference between restlessness and aches and pains. Linens are equally important; do you prefer soft flannel that keeps you warm and cozy, or do you need cooling bamboo that wicks away moisture through the night?

Light can have a significant impact on your sleep, too. It can help to invest in quality room-darkening blinds. You can reduce the light in the room by limiting electronics such as digital alarm clocks, computers, and television screens in the bedroom. Using a light that gradually dims or has an audio feature with nature sounds or white noise can also be helpful.

Keep the room temperature on the cool side. Maybe you like the window open just a bit, even in winter, or you set the thermostat lower at night. If your bedding is warm and comfortable, the fresh, cool air can help you sleep.

Preparation

It can be helpful to have a pre-sleep routine that helps you wind down mentally and physically. Stop looking at screens at least an hour before you'd like to fall asleep. The light from the screen gives your brain the cue to stay awake and alert. Your mind also stays active and can be in an alarm state because of the content you're absorbing, whether it's the news, social media controversy, or intriguing fiction you're reading.

Avoid caffeine, sugar, or heavy meals a few hours before bed as they can impact your digestive system and your nervous system, causing sleep delays or disturbances.

Shift into activities that are calming, such as taking a warm bath, drinking herbal tea, meditation, or reading something soothing. Cuddling another person, or a pet, can also calm your nervous system and help you settle down for sleep.

Keep any activity before sleep light. Consider yoga, tai chi or other such activities that offer poses and routines that are slow and gentle, easing your body into a resting state.

Consider a journaling practice at the end of each day. Perhaps you take a few moments to make a note of three things you're grateful for about the day, or about your life in general. Or you might do some free writing, letting all the stress and worries of the day flow out of your mind. Getting your thoughts onto the page can help to free you from the tension that might keep you awake. Remind yourself that you can take care of any problems tomorrow, and that you'll do a better job if you're rested.

Tactics

When you've created a peaceful, comfortable environment for sleep, and you've followed a calming routine, but you still can't sleep, there are a variety of strategies you can try to ease your mind. All of these activities offer the same sort of effect – by creating a mild distraction from your racing thoughts, your mind can finally settle.

Keep a notepad and pen by the bed. If you suddenly remember something important you need to do the next day, you can jot it down on the notepad, which may allow your mind to rest knowing you won't forget.

Read a textbook. Choose something that is interesting enough to hold your attention for a few pages, but not so interesting it will keep you interested and reading for hours.

Count sheep. Imagine sheep in an idyllic country pasture, calmly milling about as they graze. Count the sheep (or whatever you'd like to count!) and as you focus on this imaginary scene, you may just drift off.

Count backwards. We're all well trained to count from one to one hundred, so it's usually not quite enough of a distraction to help us fall asleep. If you count backwards, you can vary your approach. Try counting backwards from one hundred. If that isn't enough of a distraction, try counting backwards from two hundred by threes or sevens.

Play an alphabet game. If you don't like numbers, try naming all the foods, or all the towns that start with the letter a, then the letter b, and so on. Making such lists takes a bit of mental energy but isn't likely to be so interesting that it keeps you wide awake, riveted to the possibility of what is next.

Imagine yourself in a peaceful place. Take some time to really set the scene, using all your senses. Then imagine yourself there, safe, comfortable, and at rest. Continue to hold the sensory details in your mind, such as a gentle breeze, a pleasant smell, the sound of waves on the shore, birdsong. Whatever you find peaceful!

Listen to a guided meditation. There are numerous apps that offer free guided meditation recordings. Experiment a bit to find a few that you like. It's important that you find the voice of the guide calming, and that the words of the meditation resonate with you for the best relaxing effect. Once you find a few, make sure they're easily accessible on your device, and listen as you lay comfortably in bed.

Any of these tactics can work if you wake in the night and have trouble falling back to sleep. Sometimes we hear a noise, or we have some bodily need. Sometimes we wake from a bad dream, or we startle awake remembering something we need to do the next day. Whatever the cause of waking, all these strategies can offer the possibility of finding sleep again.

Vagus Nerve Activation

The vagus nerve runs from our brain to our gut and has branches travelling to every major organ and throughout the body. This nerve acts as a calming centre for our nervous system, in a manner similar to the way the amygdala acts as the alarm centre for our nervous system. When we're in a state of distress or alarm, activating the vagus nerve can help to counteract the alarm.

There are a number of exercises that work to activate the vagus nerve where it runs through the back of the throat. When you take a deep breath in the 4-7-8 breathing pattern, for example, the long slow exhale acts to engage the nerve as the air passes through the throat. When we sip hot liquids such as tea or soup, we have a similar result. Singing, chanting, and humming create a vibration in the throat that also activates the vagus nerve.

Some people find it helpful to apply cold when they're in distress. This may be through the act of splashing cold water on your face, a cold cloth on the back of your neck, or stepping out into cold air (or into a cold room). This sensory experience is grounding and can activate the calming system through the vagus nerve. Gentle stretching and yoga, as well as meditation can have an impact on the vagus nerve.

Additionally, you may find various massage techniques that create a swift soothing response. One example is a massage of the ear lobe, another is a hand massage where you grasp the area between your thumb and forefinger on one hand with the thumb and forefinger of the other hand and rub gently but firmly. The butterfly hug, where you cross your hands and place your fingertips on the collarbone, tapping gently alternating sides can also be very calming. These massage techniques may be done subtly in a way that others around you may not notice that you are self-soothing, even during meetings with others or on the scene, giving you a way to settle your nervous system as you face what you must.

When Things Go Wrong

Working in high-stress, trauma-exposed environments, means that it is inevitable that things will go sideways from time to time. This is true despite your knowledge, skill, and best efforts. It's just the nature of the work.

It's true that over the course of a career, we accumulate a range of tragic experiences that take a toll. We learn the real risks humans face from our environment, from one another, and from ourselves. We come to see the world differently, and it can wear us down.

It's also true that sometimes when something terrible happens, it impacts us directly. Maybe we are just a witness to horrific circumstances, maybe we are directly involved in the incident, or maybe the tragedy occurred because of our action or inaction.

Planning for Problems

Expect things to go wrong. In high stress, trauma-exposed work environments, you're dealing with things that go wrong for other people on a regular basis. It's what brings you into the incident – you're there to help solve problems and work things out. Due to the nature of the work, you're going to run a higher risk of having things go wrong when you're trying to function in a situation where something has already gone poorly. It's inevitable that you will experience crises that affect you personally over the course of a career. When you're prepared for this, it can help you cope with the experience because it will come as less of a shock that something might go sideways despite your excellent training, skill, and experience.

Expect to have a response when things go wrong. When we experience a crisis, our nervous system automatically goes into fight or flight mode. No one can avoid this automatic neurobiological process that happens within us when we detect a threat. When the crisis impacts someone else, our system can adapt quickly, allowing us to respond effectively. This is especially true as we gain knowledge, skills, and experience. However, when the incident impacts you personally, it becomes much more difficult to overcome the immediate response of your nervous system. You're only human, and our human bodies just work this way. It does not mean you are weak or broken; it means your nervous system is responding to a threat by activating its survival system, exactly as nature intended.

Prevention means knowing what calms you. It's inevitable that things will go wrong, and you'll experience a trauma response, probably several times over the course of a career. It will be particularly helpful to know what helps calm your nervous system before you face such crises. When you are regularly taking care of yourself with activities that keep you feeling well, you'll be centered and grounded on a regular basis, and this will help prevent escalating into hypervigilance or dropping into numbing in response to trauma. Additionally, you'll be able to access the relaxation response much more readily after something happens because your mind and body are used to going there. In the same way that first aid instructors insist on getting practical demonstrations right, you're developing your muscle memory so that when the time comes that you need that skill, your body knows what to do.

Have a backup plan and key trusted supports in place. There will be times when your regular strategies for self care work. You'll be able to calm your nervous system so that you can eat, sleep, and function normally in a reasonably short time. There may also be times when all your usual tactics aren't enough to soothe you. If you've got a plan that involves a solid support network, you'll be able to activate recovery more quickly. It can be helpful, for example, to have a therapist you see periodically for check-ins before you are in crisis. Having a trained professional as a neutral, supportive sounding board can be a benefit even as you navigate daily life and regular relationships. If you've got a therapist that you're already comfortable with then, in times of crisis, you will know that there is someone you already trust who can support you through the adjustment after an incident.

Debriefing

Debriefing exercises help to address the impact of a critical incident very quickly afterward. By taking the time to learn effective debriefing strategies, you can provide immediate, effective support that will help your colleagues adapt and recover after being involved in a traumatic event.

The process can happen formally and informally. Formal debriefing is important. Organizations can and should have a protocol and procedures in place to ensure debriefing happens after any call included in the Terrible Ten identified early in this text. A specially trained professional who was not involved with the incident facilitates a thorough debriefing process that includes everyone who was present and impacted. There may be two groups, with the group with direct on-scene experience is debriefed together and others who are aware of the incident and impacted are debriefed separately and without exposure to additional graphic details that may traumatize them further.

Informal debriefing happens on the fly when colleagues who experienced the same event gather at meetings or over meals. This type of debriefing can devolve into heavy drinking and sharing horror stories, which tends to be retraumatizing and unhelpful. Learning specific debriefing strategies across an organization can help team members debrief informally in safer ways.

There are a range of approaches to debriefing. Some approaches are focused on problem-solving and learning to prevent repetition of errors, and these are useful for accountability and the development of effective policies and procedures. However, when we think about wellness and resilience, we want to think of debriefing as a way to address the emotional impact and the thought processes in the aftermath of a traumatic event in order to prevent consequences such as post-traumatic stress disorder.

A good debriefing strategy that supports resilience recovery after an incident helps team members acknowledge that something difficult has happened and it's quite possible it will have an impact on them. It gives people a chance to speak aloud about the realities of a tragedy and their response to the situation. Debriefing normalizes the range of responses and reminds us that there are things we can do to take care of ourselves as we recover from our immediate response.

Debriefing can look different if it is done in a formal way during supervision or on the fly with colleagues. Important components to the process, wherever and whenever it takes place, include:

1. ***Hydration.*** Whenever possible, get some water. It will help restore balance to the system, which will help a person think and feel better.
2. ***Movement.*** Even a short walk down the hallway or around a room will help discharge some of the physical tension that builds in a crisis, which will also help reduce the mental tension.
3. ***Discussion (with warning and consent).*** It's important to be offered the opportunity to talk about what they have experienced, as it can help to accept the reality and begin to make some sense of what has happened. Some people will have more to say, and some will say less; this step is more about offering the opportunity to talk rather than trying to force someone to speak about their thoughts and feelings.

Debriefing strategies help to keep everyone **SAFER** because they:

Steady and stabilize people in the immediate aftermath of a critical incident.

Acknowledge the facts and feelings associated with the incident.

Facilitate understanding of the experience of a critical incident in the moment and in the aftermath.

Encourage adaptive coping strategies that will help calm the nervous system.

Recovery of routine functioning is supported when debriefing strategies are in place.

Recovering Resilience

Critical Incident Stress Management (CISM) offers a proven process for responding to and mitigating the impact of traumatic incidents. When there is a plan in place, your team members will benefit from this intervention, which offers education, debriefing, and support.

Beginning as soon as possible after the incident, involved team members gather to review the incident briefly, and the facilitator reminds them that they can expect to have a response to this situation that may impact them physically, mentally, emotionally, and spiritually. Often, this is also an opportunity to remind people that it is helpful to use strategies such as physical movement to discharge the tension created by the experience, intentional breathing to help regulate the nervous system, and taking care of basic needs such as hydration, nutrition, and sleep.

Within a few days, team members gather again for a fuller review of the incident. This is not a fact-finding mission, and it's not related to evaluation or discipline in any way. It's a wellness debriefing to check in with team members about their experience of the event and how they're managing their response. This is also an opportunity to offer additional support to anyone who is experiencing a significant impact because of their involvement.

Together, and when undertaken promptly, the steps in the CISM process help to

- normalize the natural response team members may have to a critical incident,

- remind them of coping skills they already use regularly,

- offer them additional strategies and support to help them process the incident and recover.

Post-Traumatic Stress Disorder

We have been hearing quite a lot about ***post-traumatic stress disorder*** for some time now. It's important to realize that our natural, automatic, neurobiological stress response during and after a traumatic experience can lead to a psychological injury that impacts our ability to function at work and in daily life. When the crisis happens, our body responds to the threat by shifting into survival mode. This is normal, a defence designed to keep us safe. The challenge comes if we get stuck in that stress response, with symptoms such as flashbacks, nightmares, intrusive thoughts, difficulty with appetite and sleep habits, and so forth. When we get stuck in these symptoms, we call it post-traumatic stress disorder. We know so much more about this now, and there are several therapies that have been shown to help someone recover, including EMDR (Eye Movement Desensitization and Reprocessing), CPT (Cognitive Processing Therapy), PE (Prolonged Exposure Therapy) and SIT (Stress Inoculation Therapy). Psychopharmacology also offers recovery support with medication options.

Post-Traumatic Growth

We're also learning more about the concept of ***post-traumatic growth***. It's true that every human has some sort of post-traumatic stress response when faced with a severe threat. We know that this response is natural. We also know that sometimes it is easily overcome while other times it is debilitating. When people receive care that includes education to normalize their response, coping strategies, and support to help them adapt after the experience, it is possible to recover. Through recovery, it is also possible to experience growth. Every crisis is an opportunity to acknowledge the very difficult aspects of being human, and to find ways to bring new meaning and purpose to life. Although you may never have chosen to live through a critical incident or tragic event, the experience may change your perspective and offer you a renewed sense of possibility as you consider what you want to do with your life. Some people take the worst thing that has happened to them and find a way to learn, grow and give back to their community in ways they might not have without this experience. This is the potential for growth, and it can impact our outlook, our habits, our goals, our relationships, and our beliefs. We have the possibility of adapting and finding our best possible life in the aftermath of trauma because of what we have learned and how we have grown through the experience.

Making Mistakes and Taking Ownership

This is a sensitive subject when we are always on our guard, trying to do our best as trained professionals who work in life and death. I'm sharing more of my personal story here, to help this concept be relevant and relatable. Through the lens of my experience, I hope you accept my invitation to reflect, without judgment, on your own.

It has always been challenging for me to admit my mistakes, despite the fact that I have had plenty of opportunities to practice.

I didn't like it when I had to take the stolen Lifesavers back to the store and pay for them, but that is how four-year-old me learned how stores work.

I was thoroughly embarrassed when, bored in religion class, I slammed my bible shut and startled the visiting teacher so much she knocked her felt board over. Our classroom teacher, a woman with a quietly stern approach to discipline, made direct eye contact with the normally very-much-a-rule-follower me as she said, "I don't know who did that, but I'm quite sure it won't happen again." It took almost two decades to release nine-year-old me from the guilt and shame associated with that incident. It was only when I was coaching nine-to-eleven-year-old soccer players that I could finally forgive myself for that "bad" behaviour, having compassion for these young players as they also learned lessons about how to get along in the world.

I remember a heated debate one day in grade seven about which actor was Bud Abbot and which was Lou Costello of the popular comedy duo. I was righteously adamant that Lou Costello was surely the tall one. In those days, well before Google, I had to wait until Saturday morning when The Abbott and Costello show was broadcast to learn that I was, in fact, wrong. Monday morning found me in class acknowledging my error. My classmate was probably about as gracious as a twelve-year-old gets, and I learned a little bit about the dangers of being aggressively righteous in expressing my thoughts and opinions.

I'm much older now, still making mistakes, still finding it difficult to acknowledge them, making amends where I can, and learning the lessons that sometimes only come from making the wrong choice.

I sometimes think about moments in time where I wish I had said or done something different. We can't "unring" a bell and there are no do-overs in these matters, but we can learn from our mistakes, and we can make the effort to make amends wherever possible.

When I was a brand-new child welfare worker, my first supervisor told me that I should expect people to complain about me and my work. If no one ever complains about you as a child welfare worker, he said, you're probably not doing your job. That was good advice that served me well as it fortified me when someone did make a complaint about me, as happened from time to time over the years.

Still, being given that piece of practical wisdom didn't mean that I dismissed people's complaints and concerns. It has been a very important part of my on-going development as a social worker to reflect on how I'm doing and how I can continue to learn, grow and do better.

When I worked assessing high conflict custody and access situations, I worked hard to present a fair and neutral report with clear evidence to support my recommendations for families. I wondered and worried at the end of every investigation whether I'd gotten it right. There were often disputes filed by the parties involved in an effort to challenge the facts of my report and my conclusions. That early advice about expecting complaints helped me reflect on the facts of the situation rather than taking a defensive stance that included outright dismissal of anyone's criticism or arguments.

I once wrote a thirty-page report and received a twenty-page dispute. When I calmed myself enough to read through the complaint, I realized that most of the document was incorrect according to the evidence I had gathered, but there was one valid point about one of the recommendations I made. Though it was rare that we would revise our reports based on the complaints we received, I maintained that we should acknowledge the one valid point in the twenty-page document. It was an oversight that could be important, and an adjustment to the recommendation was reasonable on that one point.

In ten years, I conducted more than one hundred custody and access investigations, and in twenty years as a child welfare worker, I worked with countless additional families. In all that contentious work, only one file I worked on went to trial. Every other matter was resolved some other way, and I think that, at least in part, was due to my willingness to reflect on my own actions and decisions, my ability to acknowledge where I may have made an error and to work to correct such errors whenever possible.

Once, when I'd been in private practice as a grief and trauma therapist for a few years, I'd scheduled five sessions the day I was back to work immediately after a busy and emotional trip. It was too much, and my energy was flagging by the final session of the day. I felt myself holding tension as the person spoke. I was reactive, taking their comments personally and becoming defensive. I knew immediately that I was hurting the person with my reaction. I was re-opening some of the very wounds they had come to see me hoping to heal. The session ended painfully, with both of us feeling the uneasy strain.

I wrote a letter of apology for my reactive behaviour, offering a brief explanation that I was not at my best that day. I invited them to return for a session at no cost to allow the opportunity to address the previous session, even if they chose not to continue working with me.

They accepted my invitation, and when they arrived for that follow-up session, we talked about what had happened and how they felt. I was able to validate their feelings about the session that ended poorly, and we were able to return to the topic of the session and do a bit more work on that, too.

That person let me know that receiving my note was the first time they could ever remember anyone apologizing and offering to make amends for doing them wrong. My mistake was human, and my effort to correct it made all the difference. It gave us another angle to consider in our approach to their healing journey and we went on to work together a while longer.

Sometimes, the cost of an error is very high. With training in first aid, and having worked as a first aid instructor for a few years, I came across a situation where someone was in medical distress. An ambulance was called, and I sat with the person as they gradually experienced more difficulty breathing and responding. Despite teaching people to listen for agonal breathing, a sign that someone is not receiving adequate oxygen and needs CPR, I didn't recognize agonal breathing when I encountered it for the first time in this situation. I held the person's hand, offering comfort as I could while we waited for the ambulance, when I should have started compressions and breaths. I learned several days later through a news report that the person had not survived.

This outcome weighed heavily. I knew I needed to process my thoughts and feelings. I sought out another first aid instructor I knew – one with decades of experience – and asked if they would mind talking it over with me. With their consent to debrief, I reviewed the incident explaining what had happened and what I'd done – and not done. I was reminded that the person had a significant medical condition that meant they might have died even had I performed CPR flawlessly. I remember how reassuring it was to learn that the first time this experienced first aider had encountered agonal breathing at a scene, they hadn't recognized it either. It reminded me that learning sometimes involves mistakes and failure, and that this is true for all of us. Learning occurs when we take the lesson of such an experience with us to help prevent a similar outcome in the future.

Humans make mistakes. It's inevitable. When your work involves high stakes, life-and-death situations on a regular basis, it's likely that you will err at times. If it happens, I urge you to find ways to move through the experience from the inevitable feelings of fear, doubt, guilt, regret, shame and grief toward the more healing actions of self-compassion and forgiveness. You have done the best you can, and that is all anyone can ever do, even when our best has not led to the outcome we hoped for. We can learn, rest, and try again; it is through this process that we improve. It is through this process we can go on to help many others with our knowledge, skill, and experience.

Carrying It All

I often use metaphor and analogies when I speak about trauma and grief. One of my favourites is this, the idea of the invisible backpack we all carry, that holds all the experiences of our lifetime.

When we experience a traumatic event, our mind and body automatically respond to protect us. The event triggers the survival centre of our nervous system to kick into high gear, sending out an alarm signal that shifts us into fight, flight, or freeze mode. This happens to every single human in the face of a perceived threat. When we work in high stress, trauma-exposed environments, we can experience this alarm state several times a day as we move from crisis to crisis throughout a shift. Typically, our training and experience allow us to override our nervous system's response, allowing us to respond to the situation and work to resolve the problem.

Though we may be able to function in a crisis, sometimes extremely well, we are still impacted by the automatic neurobiological response within our nervous system. Over time, our baseline changes and we may become quite vigilant about our surroundings, on alert all the time and ready to flip up into the alarm state quite readily.

It's also true that when we experience a trauma that has some personal impact, one that is outside of the usual human struggles we are trained to move into and out of throughout our shift, that it will have a powerful impact that can surprise us. After all, trauma is what we get paid to do.

The traumatic event that impacts you personally is different. Think of it as if being handed an ugly package. At first, we hold it as far away from our bodies as possible. We try not to look at it, but it's right there taking up our full field of vision as we stretch our arms out in front of us. Eventually, our arms get tired. We shift position, bending our elbows and drawing the ugly package closer to us. As we sit with this package and make these shifts, we're getting to know this package. The rips, tears and stains become more familiar. As we get used to it, we're able to bring the package closer still. It's ugly, sure. And it's ours. There is no setting it down. There is no escape, so we might as well figure out how to carry it as best we can. In time, we figure out how to hold it with one arm, propping it against our hip. This shift frees one arm and opens our field of vision. We're adapting to this real and ugly thing that is ours.

Imagine that every human wears an invisible backpack. In our backpack, we carry all the difficult experiences we've had in life. Some are small pebbles, a mere inconvenience. Some are hefty, but smooth-edged reminders of challenges we've faced and overcome, and some are weighty, with jagged edges. Ultimately, we want to move this ugly package into the backpack, too.

Once the package is safely in the backpack, we can look to the future and act with more ease. It doesn't mean we're done with the package. No, that ugly package will always be yours. Occasionally you might choose to open the backpack and look at the package, reminding yourself of what you have experienced and overcome. You might do this in therapy, or as part of teaching others how to cope with their own ugly packages. Sometimes, the backpack might spill open, and the package will tumble out and you'll have to pick it up again, taking in the ugliness, holding it, and shifting it until you can tuck it back into that trusty backpack and carry on once more. This is the process of learning to carry it all. Letting the ugly packages become just one of the things we carry instead of being the only thing we can see, think about and hold.

TL;DR Principles of Self-Preservation I Wish Everyone Knew

Take care of YOU, too. If you don't, one day you will have nothing left to give. You matter, and you must fuel that brilliant light you shine in the world.

Never stop learning. Go to conferences, sign up for training that takes you beyond the basics, learn about what you find interesting. It keeps you fresh.

Share what you know. Find a way to help others along their path as a mentor, a supervisor, a member of a peer support program, or a trainer and educator. You've learned valuable lessons you can pass on.

Embrace ethics. Do the right thing, even when no one else is looking. If you find yourself taking short cuts, it's a sign you're feeling depleted and need to get back to taking care of YOU.

Control what you can. Recognize that no matter what you're facing, you can adapt how you think about things and what actions you take. Start there, and return there, as often as necessary.

Acknowledge your mistakes. You're human, so mistakes are bound to happen. When they do, admit it, take ownership, make amends, and try not to let it happen again.

Remember, "perfect" is just a social construct. There's no such thing as being perfect. You will make mistakes. You can't please everyone. All you can do is put forth your best effort, and when your best isn't working very well, you can learn, grow, and try again.

Never stop trying. You will inevitably face hardships and times of distress. Be prepared for challenges and remember that nothing lasts forever – not the good times, and not the bad times either. Rest as you need to, but don't give up.

Try something different. If you always do what you've always done, you'll always get the same result. Be creative in your thinking, and as you look at situations from different angles you may be surprised at the solutions that appear.

Nurture courage. Do what you can to be prepared for anything AND know that you can't be prepared for every possibility. It's okay to be afraid, but don't let fear stop you from doing what's important to you.

Accept vulnerability. You're human, so you are not invincible. You may experience physical and/or psychological injuries over the course of a career. If this happens, take the time to heal. Trying to tough it out or rushing back before recovery often leads to setbacks.

Cultivate compassion. Be kind to yourself first. Even on the worst days, you're always doing the best you can. Give yourself grace when it isn't going the way you would like. When you have self-compassion, it increases your ability to have compassion for others, too.

Build relationships. Get to know your colleagues. Build rapport with the people you serve. Make connections across your community in your professional and personal capacities.

Notice the good. Even on the most difficult day, there is something to be grateful for. Maybe it's the sunshine, or much-needed rain after a dry spell. Maybe it's a smile you gave or received. When we pay attention to the little glimmers of hope and positivity it helps balance out the painful parts of life.

Access your wisdom. Pause. Breathe. Feel. Think. You know more than you think you know. If you quiet your mind and consider situations, you may realize you know just what to try next.

Trust your instincts. Your nervous system is paying attention to your environment in ways that you're not always aware of. When you have a gut feeling, or a sense about something, take note and proceed with caution.

Challenge your inner critic. While your inner critic has the important job of correcting you and keeping you on track in your day-to-day life, sometimes it takes over in a harsh, punitive way that is unproductive. When this happens, give your inner critic a time out and invite your inner cheerleader to show up with some ideas about what might help you take the next step.

Listen to your body. Try a guided meditation to scan your body from head to toe. Notice where you're holding tension. Consider what aches, pains, and ailments you've gotten used to managing. It may be your body telling you it's time for a rest, for deep self care, or medical treatment.

Remember why you started and what's gone well. What drew you to this profession? What hopes did you hold for this noble career? What are the gifts this work has given you?

Love what you do. When you're passionate about your work, it can help buffer the inevitable challenges faced in any profession. If you used to love your job and lately you're feeling stagnant, even after you've made efforts to really dig into resilience and self-preservation strategies, it may be time to make a change.

Look for opportunities that give you that spark of excitement as you think about how you can use your knowledge, experience, and skills.

When It's Time to Leave

I developed a workshop to teach people in trauma-exposed work environments about self-preservation because I knew from personal experience that surviving and thriving in your own life becomes a real challenge when you show up to help other people in crisis. This book is based on the workshop I deliver, and the strategies I offer are based on research and include the things that have helped me and so many others develop, recover, or maintain resilience across a career.

The truth is, sometimes all the strategies aren't enough, and we have to make the hard decision to leave a career that we love, that gives us identity, and may feel like the only thing we know how to do. I am sharing part of my story here to illustrate some of the experiences that led me to leave child welfare after twenty years in the field.

Every year, right before Mother's Day, she would call me to ask how the child was doing. If they were healthy, and if they were doing well in school. I would be vague and positive, no matter what was actually happening. We'd spend the rest of the call talking about what she was up to. I listened, offering her praise and encouragement. Giving up custody is hard. The ache never left her, and I heard it every year, just before Mother's Day, until I stopped working there.

Right after Mother's Day, I would have the dream. Carrying a child in each arm, frantic to escape, I was climbing an endless staircase. I could hear the clamour behind me, but I could never see the face. I knew though. I knew that it was an angry parent, coming to get their children. I could feel my lungs burning as I hoisted a child on each hip and kept running up the stairs. The children were screaming, the parent was yelling, and I was panicking. I always woke, startled and sitting halfway up with my arms out around two imagined children. My heart raced and I was clammy with the layer of sweat on my brow. It was fine. I was safe. The children were safe. The fear never left me, and I had that nightmare every year, just after Mother's Day, until I stopped working there.

The nightmares were how I knew it was time to shift roles again. From Family Service to Intake. From Intake to work at another agency – busywork, completing record checks and redacting records. Work that didn't give me nightmares, and work that I could start and finish in one day.

My restlessness grew, and like the nightmares, the disquiet signalled time for another shift. Returning to the mothership of my original agency, I found myself working on a generic team, integrating intake and family service responsibilities into one role. We did the initial intake investigations, and if the file was staying open, we carried it as the on-going worker. This strategy worked well if you developed a good working relationship during the investigation. The family would work well with the status quo. If the investigation was a nightmare, though, this style of case management left everyone struggling – the family against the worker and the worker against the family in a relentless cycle.

With my final maternity leave I thought there would be no more protection work. There was no more work at all, really. Not steady work, and not in child welfare, for another two years. But then, a return to the fold. Back to the mothership once more, but on the Resource Team this time. Reprising a role I had held for a time at a neighbouring agency, I conducted foster home assessments. I also worked with foster homes and group homes to ensure annual compliance checklists were addressed, and in-between problems got attention.

I stayed there, in that role until the merger. Across the province agencies were joining together to help reduce the massive costs of child welfare services. The decision made, our small agency was partnered with a larger one, and the wheels began to turn. The term merger feels hollow when decisions are made by a majority vote and you're on the side with smaller numbers. Our halls filled with walking wounded as our agency culture died a reluctant death.

I threw a wake for our agency, renting the little hall where we had always held our potluck holiday parties. As a slideshow with music played, colleagues present and past reminiscing over memories, connections, and the culture of our little agency operating in a county with no city.

The merger process ultimately signalled the end of my time in child welfare. After 20 years on the frontlines, I resigned. It was a big adjustment and created an identity crisis as I transitioned into private practice. I sometimes still say "We" when I refer to child welfare workers.

During my final year as a protection worker, I'd become quite ill with ulcerative colitis. The specialist said I'd need medication for the rest of my life to keep the debilitating attacks at bay. It turns out that within a year of leaving child welfare, my body recovered. I no longer take any medication, and my last colonoscopy shows no signs that my colon was ever diseased.

I do not make the suggestion to leave lightly. Though staying in a challenging work situation is not easy, leaving is very difficult, too. There are so many factors to consider, not the least of which include concerns about salary, benefits, and pension. Still, when your body is keeping score, and your health is at risk, leaving is an option that must be on the table – whether it's an internal move from one department to another, or a full career change.

Final Notes

High Stress, trauma-exposed work will change you. You will never again be the person you were, with the luxury of not knowing so much about the terrible things that can happen to humans. As you carry the stories of the ones you meet along the way, it will change how you think, feel, and act. It's inevitable.

You can, and should, make taking care of yourself a priority. The strategies suggested in this book are just a springboard from which you can create your own unique self-preservation plan. Experiment to find what keeps your sense of hope and joy alive. Know that the need to do this is natural in such a work environment.

You are not broken. You are not weak. You are having a natural reaction to the experiences you are exposed to. When you've been wounded, you can recover.

You shine a beautiful light in this world. You are always worthy of the time and energy it takes to make your wellness a priority to keep that light shining.

I've created a brief guided meditation called Shine Your Light to remind you to be gentle with yourself. You'll find a QR code and link on the resources page at the back of the book.

Gratitude

What made you smile today?
What was the best part of your week?
What do you most like to do with your free time?
What makes your life easier?
What song always lifts your mood?
Where is your favourite place to spend time?
What sentimental item do you cherish?
What is the most practical thing you own?
Who do you love spending time with?
Who shows up for you when you need help?
Who understands you best?
Who makes you laugh?
Who always remembers your birthday?
Who checks in on you?
Who shares your taste in books/music/film?
Who comforts you when you're feeling low?

What You Say to Yourself Matters: Affirmations Work

I'm doing the best I can.
I'm only human, and humans make mistakes.
I am learning.
I am stronger than I know.
It's okay not to be okay.
It's okay to ask for help.
I can change how I think about the situation.
I can take small steps towards change.
Small steps are progress.
I can face my fears.
I'm not alone.
I have good people in my corner.
I am capable of figuring this out.
I make a difference.
I am good and getting better.
I am open to change.
When I fall, I can get back up.
Failure is just an opportunity to learn.
I can overcome anything.
Every problem has a solution.
It's okay to rest.

Resources

Davis, Louanne. 2017. **Meditations for Healing Trauma**

Goldstein, Elisha and Stahl, Bob. 2016. **MBSR Every Day: Daily Practices from the Heart of Mindfulness-Based Stress Reduction**

Harris, Dan. 2018. **Meditation for Fidgety Skeptics**

Henden, John. 2017 **What It Takes to Thrive: Techniques for Severe Trauma and Stress Recovery**

Izzo, Ellie, and Miller, Vicki Carpel. **2018. Second-Hand Shock: Surviving and Overcoming Vicarious Trauma**

Levine, Peter A. 2008. **Healing Trauma: A Pioneering Program for Restoring the Wisdom of Your Body**

Mathieu, Francoise. 2011. **The Compassion Fatigue Workbook.**

Rosenberg, Stanley. 2021. **Accessing the Healing Power of the Vagus Nerve**

Rothschild, Babette. 2010. **8 Keys to Safe Trauma Recovery: Take Charge Strategies to Empower Your Healing**

Schwartz, Arielle. 2020. **The Post-Traumatic Growth Guidebook**

Winston, Sally M. and Seif, Martin N. 2017. **Overcoming Unwanted Intrusive Thoughts**

Spotify Playlist: Optimistic Vibes[1]

Shine Your Light: A brief guided meditation.[2]

---

1. https://open.spotify.com/playlist/5QXYfBXOspmgyJ1DcMxKsl?si=abf0654e804f4f73
2. https://youtu.be/lw0I2HZET84?si=yLlusW56C9oTuCxb

Acknowledgements

I am very lucky. I get to do work I love; speaking with individuals and audiences, writing books and songs, making art alone and in groups. I'm fortunate, too, that I have so many kind, generous and supportive people shining a light along my path to help me along in so many ways. As I bring this particular project to the world, my deep gratitude is extended to:

Bob McLean, for believing in me and saying it out loud *and* in writing so I would know and remember, and for helping me find my way back to writing things besides affidavits and reports;

Everyone I've met through Firefly Creative Writing: founder Chris Fraser, her fantastic team of coaches, and all of the shining hearts I have met around the table, sipping tea and sharing words – most especially the beautiful souls on screen in The Big One in 2023 and on the porch at Hearts on Fire every time;

Michelle Walker, my sister of the heart, for always being my first reader and helping me find form in the messiest state of a first draft;

Brian Knowler, Scott Hogan, Stephanie Woodward and Christie Lee for thoughtful feedback on middle drafts;

Hallie Kanuk, for offering insightful editing suggestions;

Angela Johnson, for being so awesome in so many ways, not the least of which was proofreading this text;

Jennifer Bogart, for Buttermilk breakfasts and for lending her considerable talents in book design to create a ready-to-publish manuscript;

Ron Hawkins, for finding the depths in our brief exchanges and creating brilliant images that reflect just what I hoped for.

Maureen Pollard is a registered social worker who operates a group private practice in Ontario, Canada. With more than 33 years of experience in the field, Maureen specializes in supporting people of all ages integrating grief and trauma experiences, as well as supporting first responders and frontline professionals with resilience recovery through education, critical incident support, and wellness programming. Maureen incorporates expressive arts into her therapy practice and created the Write to Heal therapeutic writing and songwriting program, as well as the Art to Heal the Heart program, offering tools everyone can use for healing and wellness.

Maureen is the author of *The Twentieth Year: A Memoir of Miscarriage*, *Best Interests: A Novel*, and *What I Wish for You*, a book of affirmations. As part of her own self-preservation and resilience strategy Maureen also writes songs, sings, and plays a little guitar. Some of her songs have been produced to raise funds and awareness for Canadian charities including the Canadian Association for Suicide Prevention and the Canadian Critical Incident Stress Foundation.

www.ingramcontent.com/pod-product-compliance
Lightning Source LLC
Chambersburg PA
CBHW060839190426
43197CB00040B/2709